Using Electronic Mail in an Educational Setting

by
Dan H. Wishnietsky

Library of Congress Catalog Card Number 91-60203
ISBN 0-87367-316-6

Bloomington, Indiana

This fastback is sponsored by the Saginaw Bay Michigan Chapter of Phi Delta Kappa, which made a generous contribution toward publication costs.

Table of Contents

Introduction

Today's students will soon find themselves in a society in which the computer will be more common than the telephone. Already, in many cities, people can bank at home, analyze the stock market, and prepare and submit tax returns using a personal computer and a modem. Examples of computer use in organizations include hospitals using computers to diagnose diseases and recommend treatments, geologists using computers to predict possible locations of mineral deposits, and travel agents using computers to secure instant reservations worldwide. The computer has quickly become one of the most powerful forces molding society, and it will have an enormous impact on the lives of our students.

Microcomputers are proliferating into all areas of our schools. They are found in most administrative offices and many classrooms. Almost every school now has a computer center. Although no one can predict the future with certainty, it is reasonable to believe that computers will be increasingly accessible to students and educators on the campus, in the workplace, and in the home.

Most of this growth in educational computing occurred in the 1980s. Teachers and administrators were trained to use microcomputers; computer software was developed for almost every area in the curriculum; and many students were introduced to computing. But the accomplishments of the 1980s were only a foundation for what will occur in the 1990s and beyond. As computer technologies become more universal, powerful, and flexible, educators must design programs that provide new opportunities to enhance learning. The challenge is to provide today's students a better education with the help of computers than they would have received without them.

Part of the always-changing field of computers is the growing use of electronic mail/message systems (EMMS), a general term for describing the transmission of messages using computers and telecommunications facilities. As the result of these advances, it is possible for administrators, teachers, staff, and students to have immediate access to personal messages, educational resources, information services, and each other – even when they are separated by great distances.

This fastback will examine how electronic mail/message systems can be used in an educational setting. The first chapter describes EMMS; and the next three chapters present its uses for administrators, faculty, and students. Chapter Five examines some of the problems that can occur when designing and implementing a telecommunications network. The final chapter attempts to predict future trends for EMMS in education and instill in the reader the importance of continually assessing the potential of technology to ensure its effective use in schools of the 21st century.

Electronic Mail/Message Systems

When computers were first used in education, every computer was separate from every other computer. If several people wanted to use the same word-processing program, each user had to have a separate disk containing the desired program. A major limitation of these stand-alone computers was the inability of one computer user to share information quickly with another user.

This changed with the arrival of computer networks, which interconnect two or more computers. Most networks in education settings are local-area networks, where a small number of computers are connected by cables to a multiplexer and a hard disk. The multiplexer permits every computer on the network to access all the programs and files stored on the hard disk. Separate copies of the program are unnecessary, because each computer on the network can communicate with the multiplexer and obtain the needed software.

The real power of sharing information, however, occurs when the computers are in different cities, states, or even countries. These computers, instead of being connected by cables, are connected by phone lines, microwave stations, or satellites. In a matter of seconds, a file from one computer can be shared with another computer located thousands of miles away. People in the tundra of Alaska can send and receive messages easily to people in New York City. Communication with people in different time zones is easier, because messages can be stored until it is a convenient time to read the message.

An electronic mail/message system (EMMS) is a network application that electronically transmits, stores, and delivers messages. Electronic mail can be compared to a post office box. The post office is open at all times, and people who have a post office box can access it at any time.

EMMS was developed because of the limitations of such other message delivery systems as the postal service and the telephone. Compared to electronic mail, the postal service is slow and sometimes undependable. The problem with the telephone is that it is not effective unless the person called can be located; and even if the person can be located, he or she may be unable or unwilling to accept the call at that time. These problems are so widespread that phrases such as "mailroom drag" and "telephone tag" are used in large organizations by people who must do a lot of communicating.

Electronic mail overcomes "mailroom drag" and "telephone tag" by its speed and its ability to store messages. Suppose Dr. Smith, the superintendent of a school system, needs to send a message to two school principals, Ms. Clark and Mr. Jones. Dr. Smith types the message and sends it to Ms. Clark's and Mr. Jones' "mailbox" on the computer network. The message is immediately stored in Ms. Clark's and Mr. Jones' "mailbox" for future retrieval. If Ms. Clark is using her computer when the message is sent, the computer notifies her that she has mail. When it is convenient, Ms. Clark reads the message and responds appropriately. If Dr. Smith's message to Mr. Jones arrives while he is having a conference with a parent, he does not have to be interrupted, because the message has been stored. Later when he checks his computer, Mr. Jones is notified that there is a message in his mailbox. He retrieves it at his convenience and executes any warranted reply.

There also are national networks that link many thousands of computer users. Two major personal computing/communication network organizations are The Source and CompuServe Information Service. Both of these networks offer an electronic mail system that allows any individual with a personal computer and a modem to exchange messages with any other person on the network. Each network charges a subscription fee and a usage fee, which varies with the time of day. Access to these communication networks also allows instant access to many other information and communications services.

There are a variety of methods for transmitting messages electronically. Following are descriptions of some of them.

Message Distribution Services

Message distribution services transmit a keyed or spoken message by electronic means. Advantages include the ability to send messages at any time without having to locate or interrupt the receivers, the storage of messages so receivers can access their messages at their convenience, and the capability to retransmit messages to others on the network.

Another benefit is the ability to send the same message as easily to a selected group of people as to one individual. People on the network can be identified by categories, such as principals, math teachers, or department chairs. If the state superintendent wants to send a message to all district superintendents, he or she just addresses the message to "district superintendents." The message is placed electronically in every superintendent's computer mailbox. The superintendents can read the message at their convenience and decide whether to send a response, print the message with the computer's printer, retransmit the message to others on the network, or delete the message.

Voice Mail

Some electronic mail/message systems are equipped to handle spoken communications. The procedure is similar to the systems that transmit keyed messages except that the sender calls the voice-mail system and speaks the message. The sound waves are then converted to digital pulses and stored on a hard disk for later retrieval. The receiver hears the message, which is produced as reconstituted speech. As with typed messages, the receiver can then save the message for future reference, forward the message to another person, or delete the message.

An example of voice mail is an application used by many large banks. A depositor telephones the bank's computer, and the computer will tell the depositor information about his or her account using reconstituted speech. Vendors that serve education accounts also use voice mail. If a school administrator calls the vendor and the person being called is not available, the message is stored as digitized speech. The salesperson can check the voice mail using any touch-tone telephone.

Document and Picture Transmission

This function of EMMS entails sending a facsimile of an original document by electronic means using a fax machine or personal computer. When using fax machines, the sending fax scans the original document and translates the document to signals that are transmitted through phone lines. The receiving fax then retranslates the signals and produces a duplicate of the original.

It also is possible to use personal computers to communicate with any standard fax machine. Features include the ability to send faxes without human interaction, automatic redial when the phone line is busy, and automatic logging of incoming and outgoing faxes. Faxes also can be received by computer without interrupting any work being done on the computer. The incoming fax is automatically stored on the computer's hard disk for later viewing or printing.

Computer Conferencing

Computer conferencing permits a group to hold a conference when it is convenient for each individual. Suppose 50 principals throughout Texas wish to discuss the topic "Sexism in American Education." Instead of driving or flying to a specific location, the "conference" can be accomplished electronically by computer.

Because the messages can be stored, all the participants do not have to be at their computers at the same time. When it is convenient, each principal can call up the comments of the other principals, make additional comments, ask questions, or respond to questions. Several people can even talk at the same time, and the computer will record all discussions. After the conference is completed, a complete transcript of the discussion can be transmitted to all participants.

Administrative Uses of EMMS

This section describes different operations of electronic mail/message services that will enable school administrators to perform their jobs more quickly and more efficiently. The suggested applications will make such daily tasks as collecting data or sending memos less of a chore, thus allowing more time for thinking and making decisions. EMMS applications also aid the decision-making process through computer conferencing, database access, and data analysis.

Sending and Receiving Data

Attendance figures, achievement-test scores, grades, student addresses, and teacher salaries are all examples of frequently used data in schools. Often these data are recorded in one location, sent to another where they are combined with other data, and again transcribed before being sent to a third locale. This process might be repeated several times before each person who needs a copy of the data receives it. An example is attendance data. Every morning each homeroom teacher sends a list of absentees to the principal's office. The secretary combines the lists, rewrites the information, and sends the integrated list to the superintendent's office. The superintendent's office then has to combine the lists from each school before sending the data for the school district to the state department of education.

EMMS, used with a database management system, can eliminate the redundancy that occurs when the same data have to be written several times. Using the previous example, the homeroom teacher enters the attendance data for the class into a computer and transmits them to the principal's computer using electronic mail. The principal's computer, using the database management system, combines the attendance information without having to retype the data. The combined report then can be electronically mailed to the state education department, where it is combined with the data from the other schools in the district before being sent to the state superintendent's office. At any point in the process, the computer can print a hard copy of the data or save the data on a disk.

Another example of the benefits of EMMS is in reporting grades. Often a student's grade is written in at least three places: the teacher's grade book, the report card, and the official transcript. But the classroom teacher can enter the grade into the computer, and the computer can print the teacher's grade book and the student's grade report. The grades then can be transmitted to the registrar's office and electronically added to the student's transcript.

Message Distribution

Because their responsibilities often require them to be away from their office, school administrators frequently play the telephone-tag game. Telephone tag can be especially frustrating when the message is received too late to be of value. Many times school administrators miss meetings or conferences because a message was not delivered in a timely manner. Using campus mail or the school's courier service does not solve the problem, because campus mail can be slow and messages can be lost.

EMMS is able to distribute messages at any time in a matter of minutes to one person or a group of people and to store the message until accessed by the receiver. This is especially helpful in situations that require quick action. Suppose the budget office of a school system discovers that $50,000 in Title III money needs to be spent within two days or the money is forfeited. The budget office can type the pertinent information on the computer and send the message to the appropriate people. Anyone who receives the message could then forward the message to anyone else. The people to whom the message is addressed will be notified of the message as soon as they check their computers. After reading the message, an answer with the required information can be electronically mailed back to the budget office. There is no telephone tag or mailroom drag, and no one had to try to locate the recipients.

Using a computer that is fax-compatible also can assist the school administrator. There are occasions when a school administrator desires to send a message that already is typed, such as a vendor's specification sheet, an illustration, or a journal article. The document simply is scanned and transmitted to any fax machine or fax-compatible computer. Once the document is received and stored on a computer disk, the document can be transmitted to any other computer on the network. This allows lengthy or complicated documents to be shared without any typing by the sender.

Computer Conferences

Effective school administrators seek out the opinions of others when making important decisions. But often the exchange of views about important decisions does not occur because people cannot be at the same place at the same time. The computer conference eliminates both of these problems by enabling an administrator to confer easily with other people on the network without inconveniencing any participant.

It also is possible to obtain helpful information about a topic by posing a message or a request on an electronic bulletin board. This component of computer conferencing allows all users to share topics of common interest. Suppose a superintendent is asked to give a presentation regarding opportunities for women to coach male sports teams at the high school level. The superintendent could place a message on the electronic bulletin board requesting other superintendents or high school principals to send information about women coaching male teams. The message also would have the superintendents' electronic mailbox number. Any person with access to the bulletin board could read the message and send a reply. After the reply is received, the electronic mail function could be used for further correspondence.

Accessing Databases

Databases are libraries of information stored in a central computer. These libraries can be accessed through such networks as The Source or CompuServe and can provide the administrator with quick and easy access to useful information.

The three major database services used by educators are Dialog Information Services, Bibliographic Retrieval Services, and SDC Information Services. The largest system is the Dialog Information Services, which gives the user access to about 200 databases in such fields as government, health, education, social and physical sciences, and the humanities. The Bibliographic Retrieval Services accesses more than 60 data banks that contain abstracts from books, newspapers, magazines, and professional journals. The SDC Information Services has more than 70 databases, many duplicating those found in the Dialog Information Services.

Follow-Up Services

It is good practice to use a letter, phone call, or visit to remind or to reinforce the intent of some previous communication or action. Such follow-up activities are time consuming; and because administrators are busy, they often don't follow up. For example, an assistant superintendent for curriculum reads an article about a computer-based reading program that claims dramatic improvement in the reading levels of fifth- and sixth-graders. The assistant superintendent considers ordering the reading program, but decides first to check out the claims. She sends an electronic message to the program's publisher asking for more information and the names of schools that currently use the program. She then uses EMMS to contact the schools using the program and requests an evaluation. She also can place a message on an electronic bulletin board requesting evaluations. With the information received, an informed decision regarding the software's purchase can be made. If the software is purchased and used, EMMS will permit the fifth- and sixth-grade reading teachers to transmit their opinions of the program to the administrator. These and other EMMS follow-up procedures are performed quickly; but more important, they enhance the educational process.

Faculty Uses of EMMS

The primary function of an electronic mail/message service is communication. With an EMMS, faculty members will be able to communicate with each other more easily, access appropriate databases, do cooperative research, and transmit or receive data and text. These operations help strengthen the teaching process by increasing the teacher's sense of responsibility toward the student, encouraging strong professional associations among teachers, and facilitating the growth of theory and knowledge in teaching.

Communicating with Other Faculty

Excellent teachers often produce quality products and services that can help other teachers. Examples of these products and services include lesson plans, community projects, new curricula, learning projects, modes of instruction, and art or music programs. Some of this information is shared by word of mouth, through newsletters, or through professional journals; but many excellent ideas and activities never travel beyond the classroom door. With the electronic bulletin board, teachers can share with others on the network. These messages can be categorized by subject, grade, or any other criterion.

Some professional organizations already use electronic bulletin boards to allow their members to exchange information 24 hours a day. One of these bulletin boards, MATHLINK, is sponsored by the National Council of Teachers of Mathematics (NCTM). NCTM also has an electronic mailbox, accessed through CompuServe, for receiving "mail" from its membership.

Phi Delta Kappa's Center on Evaluation, Development, and Research (CEDR) also has an electronic bulletin board that can be accessed on SpecialNet, the largest education-oriented computer-based network in the United States. Using this bulletin board, educators may obtain information about publications, workshops, and other services available from Phi Delta Kappa. Phi Delta Kappa also has an electronic mailbox on CompuServe.

Using a national network, a teacher can contact directly a teacher in another part of the country. Suppose a geography teacher in Florida is teaching about New England. The teacher places a message on the electronic bulletin board requesting a willing teacher in New England to be part of a student postcard exchange. A geography teacher in New England who is teaching about the Southeast contacts the Florida teacher through the network, and soon the students are sharing postcards and learning about one another.

Cooperative Research

Electronic mail/message services can facilitate cooperative research by making people, relevant information, and computer applications more accessible. For example, two teachers in different states can share data and results from a study on which they are collaborating. They also can write their article together on the computer network by electronically transmitting their drafts. Instead of spending weeks exchanging drafts and revisions through the mail, the teachers can co-write their article in hours using EMMS.

Accessing Databases

Databases, such as those accessed through The Source or CompuServe, provide teachers with a wealth of information. These databases fall into three categories: statistical, bibliographical, and computational.

Statistical databases provide current information that can be used in the classroom. By the time many textbooks are published and in use, much of the statistical information is dated. Since statistical databases are updated continually, teachers and students can obtain the most current information within a few minutes.

Bibliographical databases provide instant access to newspapers, magazines, and professional journals. When a class is studying the United States government, the students and teacher using EMMS have convenient access to Washington newspapers. Business classes have access to such information as U.S. government statistical documents. There also are bibliographical databases for health, education, social science, physical science, and the humanities.

Computational databases allow users to manipulate data and produce statistical reports. The computer can sort the data and perform calculations many times faster than a human. Teachers who are doing research are able to complete the statistical portion of the research more quickly and easily and also can use the computer to create tables and charts.

Databases do not have to be national in scope. Educators can create their own databases for local use. One example is a campus calendar or campus news system. Yet another local database is the permanent records of students. When advisors have computer access to a student's permanent record, it is easy to verify what courses have been taken and what grades were earned. This will help prevent advisement errors, such as placing students in courses for which they do not have prerequisites, which will have to be corrected later.

EMMS also can be used for communicating between students and faculty outside the classroom. For example, a teacher might create a database containing assignments, practice test questions, or discussion questions. The student accesses the teacher's database and works the assignment on the computer and transmits it back to the teacher. The teacher, in turn, reviews the student's work, thus providing immediate feedback in the form of praise, corrections, or further things to think about.

Student Uses of EMMS

Perhaps the most important use of EMMS is in the teaching-learning process. This section suggests a few ways students can use EMMS for assignments, discussions, study sessions, extracurricular activities, and recreation. All the suggestions emphasize the sharing of work, student preparation, student review, student access, and telecommunications skills. By working together, students and teachers can think of many creative ways to use EMMS to achieve instructional goals.

EMMS in the Curriculum

Mathematics. Students in schools in different parts of the country could research the price of certain products in their local area. They could then share their data via EMMS and report the results using calculations at their level of mathematical skill. For example, younger students might use addition or subtraction to compare the cost of the items in the different areas of the country. Older students can calculate the percentage difference and develop charts and graphs to report the results.

English. Students can critique books, plays, and events in the community and share them with students in different schools. The best critiques might be published in a jointly developed literary magazine. The students also could place their creative writing on the network for critiquing and publication in the literary journal.

Science. Students from different schools can record and share specific weather data and compare daily average temperatures from different sections of the country. The results could be recorded on charts and graphs. The National Weather Service sponsors a program of this type. Chemistry and physics classes could share the results of laboratory experiments and work together to interpret the outcomes. Several schools could run contests such as "name the enzyme," with a clue added each day until the chemical is identified. The student who correctly names the chemical selects the next enzyme.

Social Studies. Students can use the computer to develop a travel brochure of their region to share with students from other parts of the country. The brochure could include demographics, climate, geographic features, and points of interest. The brochure also could include information about the area's prominent citizens, local celebrations, and local history.

Music. Students who enjoy different types of music could share the reasons for their musical tastes with students who enjoy other types of music. Students could write advertising copy for musical events at their school and transmit the advertisement to other local schools. After the event, the students could interview the performers and write reviews of the production to share with other students on the network.

Foreign Language. Students from different schools can jointly develop a calendar of special days and holidays of the country whose language they are studying. Travelogues of different countries also could be developed. If a school is hosting a foreign exchange student, the exchange student can use EMMS to communicate with students in other schools.

Homework. Students could develop review sheets covering different topics. These sheets could be reviewed by several students and entered into the network's database. Students also could have an online tutorial program during specific hours. If a student is having a problem with an assignment, students who have taken the course can be computer tutors. This project could involve several schools, with the tutor and student communicating by computer.

EMMS and Extracurricular Activities

Newspaper and Literary Journal. Most schools publish a school newspaper and literary journal. With electronic mail, these publications can become citywide, statewide, or national in scope. Each school could have an editor and staff who make editorial decisions and writing assignments. The articles are then shared by electronic mail with the other schools involved, and online editorial decisions are made. An areawide paper or journal is then compiled and distributed to all the schools involved. The publication could also be sent to schools on the network that were not involved with this project but might be interested in future projects.

Databases. Students can prepare databases to share with students at other schools. For example, high school students could develop an education database. Students would request information from area colleges, universities, and trade schools. The information would be placed on the network to be accessed by anyone on the network. As more schools completed this project, the database would become more comprehensive.

Students also could compile a job-market database. They would contact the personnel offices of companies in the area to discover career and part-time job opportunities. The information is placed on the network by job category and updated weekly. Some employers, once they hear about this type of database, actually call to have their jobs listed. The database could include type of job, rate of pay, working hours, and whom to contact. If the employer and the school can communicate electronically, the employer could update the database with new information regularly. A special summer and holiday job section is also useful.

Database calendars help bring together students with similar interests. School clubs and student government associations can place their calendar of events on the computer network and have a computer mailbox for messages. Managers of sports teams can develop a database containing the team's schedule, team record, and individual performances.

Competitions. Many types of games and competitions are possible on EMMS. For example, teams from different schools can debate each other using the computer. The topic is placed on the electronic bulletin board, and each school is given a specific time and word count for the debate. The format is the same as face-to-face debates, with each school presenting an opening statement, rebuttals, and closing statements. Students from non-competing schools could evaluate the arguments and determine the winning team.

Other types of games or contests for computer users could include trivial pursuit, chess, and stock exchange. Trivial pursuit and chess would be played like the board games. Players could be online or the questions and moves can be stored. Stock exchange is a computer simulation. Each player starts with a certain amount of money and trades New York Stock Exchange stocks for a period of time. The prices of the stocks are updated each day so the students know the value of their accounts. At the end of the time period, the player whose account is worth the most wins.

Personal Communications. Students should be encouraged to use electronic mail/message services for personal projects. Elementary school students enjoy exchanging telephone numbers and calling one another. By using a database and EMMS, they could create a telephone directory of electronic mail addresses on the computer and then establish computer penpals in different schools. Other examples of personal communications for elementary school students include computer games, writing letters to Santa Claus, and accessing online magazines created especially for young people.

Older students can use EMMS to help them and their families with real-life situations. For example, if the family of an eighth-grader is planning a vacation over the Christmas break, the student could help plan the itinerary using a public network. He or she would access the network to verify airline schedules and fares, hotel availability, local activities, and restaurants in the area. The student's parents could then use the information to request reservations and plan their trip.

High school students can use EMMS for securing information about choosing a college. Students can request information about admission requirements and course offerings and can transmit letters of introduction to individual professors prior to arriving on campus. College students can use EMMS in the same manner when investigating graduate schools.

High school and college students also can use EMMS to establish professional contacts. For example, all major companies and many smaller ones can be contacted using electronic mail. Students who are seeking employment can communicate with the company and inquire about job openings, job requirements, salary, and advancement opportunities. This not only provides the student with information, but also shows the company that this prospective employee has computer skills.

One of the extra benefits of personal EMMS communications are the friendships that develop. Many students become not penpals but "keyboard pals." They share information about their schools, politics, and lifestyles. After communicating via EMMS for some time, it is not uncommon for students to arrange personal visits with their keyboard pals.

Problems of EMMS

Although computers and EMMS have great potential for education, they are not without their problems. Such problems include cost, maintenance, training, access, and supervision. This section discusses some of these problems and suggests some solutions.

Cost-Related Problems

Any educator involved with a school budget knows that it is expensive to operate and maintain computers. Beyond the basic cost of computers, additional costs for EMMS include cables, other hardware, software, and charges for using telephone lines and subscriptions to networks. And with the extra hardware needed for EMMS, there is more equipment to maintain and repair. Computers are expensive but cost effective if used properly. Budget constraints may prevent the installation of a complete system, but remember that one computer with one modem can be the beginning of an effective EMMS.

Educators should not try to justify EMMS with the argument that "every school should have one." It is vital to have a plan in place detailing how the EMMS will be used and how it will enhance school operations and the curriculum. The plan should include such details as how current hardware can be incorporated into the EMMS, how the computers on the EMMS can be scheduled effectively, and which EMMS functions will most effectively meet the school's needs. Having a plan in place will lessen the chances of spending more money later to correct mistakes.

Before recommending any purchases, obtain as much information as possible. Do not rely on information from just one vendor. Contact other schools that already have installed EMMS to find out what equipment they use and their opinions about the system. Those who have had experience with EMMS are likely to know about any problems associated with particular hardware and software.

Other ways to save money include obtaining educational discounts, buying in bulk quantities, teaching students to use computers properly to avoid repair costs, training teachers and students to do minor repairs, and buying a service contract.

Funds may be procured by submitting grant proposals, conducting fund-raising projects, and enlisting the support of local businesses. Businesses often upgrade their older computer equipment with newer models. If they are aware of the school district's need, local businesses might be willing to donate the older, but often usable, computer equipment to schools and colleges. The business receives a tax deduction and the school receives needed equipment.

Usage Problems

To incorporate EMMS into the curriculum and administrative process will require thorough training of those who will use it. It is imperative that the planning of EMMS include a training component. Inservice workshops where educators receive hands-on experience are especially effective for learning about EMMS. Workshop leaders should provide technical competence and be able to deal with problems that might arise. In one workshop, teachers of certain subjects might be matched with their counterparts in another school already using EMMS. They can share information about themselves, their classes, and their ideas about teaching. Another workshop might introduce school administrators to the benefits of EMMS for administrative functions. With the experience gained in these initial workshops, more specialized training sessions can be scheduled later.

There are always some teachers and administrators who resist new technology, fearing that it depersonalizes the process of education. Their concerns must be addressed honestly. Emphasize that the computer and EMMS are tools, which, if properly used, can increase efficiency, enhance instruction, and encourage creative thought. The best way of overcoming resistance to new technology is through familiarity with it. As educators become more knowledgeable about the uses of EMMS, they will come to see it as a tool that helps them to do their job more effectively.

Students are much less likely to be resistant to EMMS. Once they have been introduced to it, most are enthusiastic and beg to use it. Then the major problem becomes one of access to the limited EMMS equipment available. One possible solution for increasing access is to place all EMMS computers in a designated resource room or lab. Teacher aides, parent volunteers, or older students might be recruited to serve as lab supervisors during the late afternoon and evening hours. Not only does this allow more time for student access, but transmission costs are usually lower after 5:00 p.m.

Ethical and Equity Issues

The widespread use of computers has created a new set of ethical issues. As computer use increases in the educational setting, students, faculty, and administrators will be confronted with such issues as privacy, destruction and theft of information, alteration of data, viruses, and other computer crime. Along with the many benefits EMMS offers is the potential for computer misuse.

Educators have the responsibility of teaching computer ethics. This should be done by both word and deed. When students observe school personnel illegally copying software or illegally accessing one of the online data retrieval systems, the wrong message is being communicated.

In addition to teaching computer ethics, schools must protect their data from unauthorized access. School databases that contain student grades, teacher salaries, standardized test scores, and other confidential information must be carefully protected. Most computer networks and EMMS have security safeguards; but it seems that as soon as safeguards are invented, ways to bypass them are soon forthcoming. There have been many incidents of students with home computers and modems gaining unauthorized entry into a school's database and altering low grades.

One safeguard is to separate the storage unit containing administrative files from the storage unit for student use. When the files are on the same storage unit, it is easier for unauthorized users to break security codes and enter classified files. When the storage units are separate, the illegal user must first gain entry to the storage unit before accessing the file. Another safeguard is to limit EMMS entry to the administrative storage unit by not having telephone access. This means that if a computer is not connected to the storage unit by cables, files stored on the unit cannot be accessed. This limits the EMMS's versatility, but it also protects the files. If telephone access is required, the telephone line can be disconnected when not in use and reconnected when needed.

Backup copies of all files should be made daily. Most EMMS security systems make a record not only when the system is accessed but also when a user tries to access the system but fails. If the system logs several failed attempts to enter the system and then a successful entry, there is a high probability that a person gained unauthorized entry. By having backup copies, any unauthorized changes can be quickly rectified and the system passwords can be changed to prevent further breach of security. Making backup copies is also appropriate policy because the files on the storage unit can be lost or damaged by power surges, disk contamination, or human error.

Another issue that school administrators must address is the matter of equity regarding access to computers and EMMS applications.

Many educators have expressed concern that we are developing two classes of people: the computer literate and the computer illiterate. This problem stems from the disparity between economically advantaged schools systems, which can afford to purchase more and better computer systems, and poorer school systems, which have difficulty providing just the basics. Also, parents of students in affluent school districts are more likely to provide needed equipment to the schools through the PTA and to have a computer equipped with an EMMS in the home.

It is beyond the scope of this fastback to resolve this equity issue, except to point out that it is one that must be addressed if we expect to develop a computer-literate citizenry.

Future Trends

To serve the needs of students into the next century, educators must plan for the future. Even without a crystal ball to predict the future, it is possible to develop long-range plans based on current trends. This section discusses these trends and suggests some possible directions for EMMS in the years ahead.

Worldwide Communications

The time of the stand-alone computer will soon be past. Already technology exists for worldwide communications networks. Dozens of satellites now orbit the earth transmitting both domestic and international communications. These satellites are monitored by INTELSAT, a consortium of about 130 member nations. And as the costs for this technology decrease, schools will be able to link into the networks via EMMS.

Currently, budget constraints limit the widespread use of long-distance communication systems in most schools. This will change as costs come down. Already several state university systems have their own cables and microwave stations for long-distance communications. In the 21st century it will be as easy and cost effective to call another country as it is to call another state.

As the cost of EMMS comes down, professional journals and organizations can become international in scope. Research will become increasingly global in nature as researchers from different nations collaborate on projects through EMMS. Instead of mailing manuscripts and letters using the postal service, it will be almost as easy to communicate with a person from another country as it is with a colleague down the hall.

Education organizations will use EMMS to create international information networks that will offer their members periodicals, research reviews, and seminars. Members will be able to exchange information, opinions, and ideas among themselves and with the organization's staff. Already, the Association of Research Libraries has collaborated with CAUSE and EDUCOM, the two leading organizations promoting computing in higher education, to form the Coalition for Networked Information. Its first project was to identify databases and make them available to educators through computer networks.

A Multicultural Curriculum

Today people from other countries are not only living in the United States, they are building factories, hiring American workers, and serving as managers in their U.S. factories. Many Americans are now working for companies owned by Japanese, British, French, and Arabic investors. To prepare students to participate in an increasingly global economy, the schools must provide a multicultural curriculum. EMMS has a vital role to play in this curriculum.

With EMMS, students in social studies classes studying the governments of other countries will be able to interact with students from those countries concerning their political processes. The students also can discuss their opinions of each other's country, world events, and personal concerns. Other classes will incorporate similar projects as schools from one country establish joint ventures with schools from other countries.

Conclusion

Not since the inventions of the Industrial Revolution has technology had the potential to transform society as the computer and telecommunications do today. Just as gears, motors, and engines extended industrial power, computers and EMMS extend thinking power. Who would have believed in 1903, when the first airplane flew for 12 seconds, that less than a century later the New York City airports alone would handle more than 12,000 flights weekly. Worldwide computer networks will accomplish similar changes as this generation enters the Information Age.

Experts report that information and knowledge is doubling every five or six years. Some predict that with increasingly powerful computers and information systems, scientific knowledge will double every two years. What better argument is there for the need for lifelong learning and computer literacy? People who do not know how to use computers will be as lost in tomorrow's world as people who do not read are left behind in today's.

Schools must prepare today's students for the technological environment they will encounter as adults. It is by continually assessing the technological landscape and its implications for learning that educators will be able to ensure that the curriculum being designed today will prepare students for the 1990s and beyond. By understanding computer technology, students will be able to control it, integrate it into their lives, and use it humanely.

EMMS Resources

Journals

Classroom Computer Learning, 5615 W. Cermak Road, Cicero, IL 60650.

Computers, Reading, and the Language Arts, P.O. Box 13039, Oakland, CA 94661.

Educational Communication and Technology Journal, 1126 Sixteenth Street, N.W., Washington, DC 20036.

Educational Computer Magazine, P.O. Box 536, Cupertino, CA 95015.

Electronic Learning, 730 Broadway, New York, NY 10003.

Teaching and Computers, P.O. Box 645, Lyndhurst, NJ 07071.

The Computing Teacher, University of Oregon, Eugene, OR 97403.

The Journal of Computers in Mathematics and Science Teaching, P.O. Box 4455, Austin, TX 78765.

Associations

Association for Computers in Mathematics and Science Teaching, P.O. Box 4, Austin, TX 78765.

Association for Educational Communications and Technology, 1126 Sixteenth Street, N.W., Washington, DC 20036.

Association for Educational Data Systems, 1201 Sixteenth Street, N.W., Washington, DC 20036.

Computers, Reading, and Language Arts, P.O. Box 13039, Oakland, CA 94661.

International Council for Computers in Education, Department of Computer and Information Science, University of Oregon, Eugene, OR 97403.

Online Sources

CompuServe Information Service, 5000 Arlington Center Blvd., P.O. Box 20212, Columbus, OH 43220.

Dialog Information Services, Inc., 3460 Hillview Avenue, Palo Alto, CA 94304.

SpecialNet, GTE Education Services, 2021 K Street, N.W., Washington, DC 20006.

The Source, 1616 Anderson Road, McLean, VA 22102.

Resource Centers

Microcomputer Resource Center, Teachers College, Columbia University, New York, NY 10027.

Minnesota Educational Computing Consortium, 2520 Broadway Drive, St. Paul, MN 55113.

Technical Education Research Centers, Computer Resource Center, 8 Eliot Street, Cambridge, MA 02138.